The Crucible of Redemption

CARLYLE MARNEY

The Crucible of Redemption

CHANTICLEER PUBLISHING COMPANY, Inc.

WAKE FOREST, NORTH CAROLINA

THE CRUCIBLE OF REDEMPTION

International Standard Book Number 0-913029-04-1

Chanticleer Publishing Company, Inc.
Box 501
Wake Forest, North Carolina 27587

To

James A. Berry

*across two decades he set
our proclamation to the music
of devotion and action in classic
liturgy—and more, lived as brother*

Preface

Nor was this little fourth volume intended as a book. Once again, these are sermons for Holy Week. They were born, almost without conscious preparation, as a daily happening, an oblation poured out, as we relived Holy Week at Myers Park Church. They belong there, in that setting of classic worship celebrated in that season of memory, expectation, participation, and hope.

Now that I no longer must do this daily, or even every week, I find I do not miss the agony of coming to some focus of proclamation regularly. Instead, I am caught up in a broader necessity, a larger sacrament, which requires me to live out the celebration I have talked about twenty-eight years. As I look back, all my proclamation seems to have participated in Advent or Easter, or somewhere in between. Perhaps this is a proper gospel. I have bet my life so. But if anyone back there had told me I must find eighty Holy Week sermons for every ten-year stance, I should have despaired. These are among those that happened as I ran. And some days, in the act of proclamation, the glory of the Lord, I think, came up on me from behind.

CARLYLE MARNEY

Contents

The
Crucible
of
Redemption

Company of Betrayers

When they said to him, "Lord, who is it that betrayeth thee?" he said, "He that dippeth his hand with me in the dish, the same shall betray me."

For me, now, there is something unreal about the Judas story. Its parts are too neatly woven into the fabric of the main event. It has a phony feel. It is as if someone who has to be explained is at last explained away. It sounds as if a crime has to be found to go with some horrible detail in the tapestry, to justify the detail. The Judas story fits too nicely into that panoramic 40 percent of Matthew given over to Holy Week. It is as if someone we did not like is tagged with something that makes our distaste look good. The story feels sick. The whole Judas episode is like something out of *Lord of the Flies*, like something out of Sartre's *Respectful Prostitute*. It makes the observer ask, "Who is the real victim here? Jesus? Or Judas?" For of a truth someone is being disposed of here. He is being disposed of so utterly that the only animal that bears his name is the wether used in abattoirs to lead flocks of sheep up to the slaughter line.

The company of the faithful is washing its hands of somebody. We get earlier tell-tale glimpses. Someone is being set up here. A character has been created for us, a character that required betrayal as its climax. Looking back over its shoulder, after the cross, and with Judas' terrible death to explain away, the Church says, "You know we never did trust him, really." And John says in his Gospel, "I think he was stealing from us all along." So there is no defense for Judas; no way to sweeten it up; no defense by ignorance; no defense because of his disappointment; no defense because of some deep motivation or weakness. There simply are no words we can put in Judas' mouth to justify. There is really no way we can get inside him. At no point are we ever permitted to look inside him. The Church sealed him shut. The early Church encapsulated him. It sealed him as the corpse of Attila was sealed—in lead and dropped in a river. There is no way to get Judas back onstage.

All the literary attempts to re-create him and explain him, even Dorothy Sayers' beautiful attempt to give him Cockney language and character, all these attempts are really empty. In Matthew and in John, Judas is sealed off. There is no way to clean him up. He is finally and fully excommunicate—the door to the return for Judas is brass and impenetrable, and there is something staged about it.

He really didn't have very much money at his disposal. All he could have had was a little grocery money for some peasant disciples. The forces who wanted Jesus under arrest needed no help to find him; they knew where he was every hour of every day that week. The betrayal kiss isn't really necessary to the story. Everybody knew the teacher. There was no real chance to mistake him, I think. It is as if, beginning with that lonely body twisting at its rope's end across some little trail, they disposed of their memory of a greater betrayal. You see, it is such an anticlimactic episode—the death of the betrayer— such a minor incident in the whole pattern of the drama of betrayal on Golgotha. (They noticed it at the time no more than we noticed the hanging of a lonely old Negro man from a limb so close to the ground that he could have stood up anytime he wanted to live. This minor incident in the drama of a betrayed race drew six lines in a south Georgia paper.) But later as they worked back over their recollections of one they never really liked, they used the Judas-death to cover their recollection of a deeper shame.

The Christian Church, I charge, has used Judas! We have our mileage out of Judas. He has been treaded and retreaded—how we have used him! Don't you see it too? Judas is there to cover something. Judas is a scapegoat for them, as for us. Judas is there to make us forget something. He is there to provide a contrast by which we look good. Judas is a screen to keep from view our agonizing awareness of the Church's original nature which we can hardly stand. *Judas is woven in, in scarlet, to keep the pale green and sickly vomitus of the infant Church's infidelity from showing too well in the tapestry.* For over against all the Judas story as counterpoint theme, woven through the great tapestry of our history, are those terrible, terrible words which are the real text today: "Then the disciples *all forsook him and fled.*"

This, not Judas, is the Church's real shame. This is the real company of betrayers: "He that dippeth his hand with me in the dish, the same shall betray me." *They all had their hands in that dish.* And they left their little brother Judas with peanut butter on his face to be their guilty party. And more, they were willing for little brother Judas to continue to bear their great guilt; and worse, so are we willing for Judas to be perpetually lost out there somewhere like the dead body of some original Russian space-man, still in orbit through centuries with our ad-vanced space vehicles passing him by.

I have written an aphorism: If Jesus died for the sins of the world, Judas died for the sins of the Church. If Jesus died for the sins of the world, Judas has been killed for us disciples.

I have a question. Can we ever be saved without our little brother Judas?

It was, and is, all so perfectly natural. There was a dramatic precedent for this—because, you see, Israel had always had two scapegoats. This may be the real symbolism we have missed. Judas is not the original betrayer; Judas is not the primal betrayer; Judas is only the typical betrayer. His betrayal is no more vicarious than Christ's suffering was vicarious. For neither the death of Judas nor of Jesus has stopped our betrayal or our suffering. But we had two scapegoats then, and we have a second one still. Israel always did have two. The tradition is as old as Ex-odus. The one unblemished lamb, a he-lamb, spotless, of perfect conformation, fed on milk all his life, with his throat cut on the altar—and they had another lamb, the one who bore their guilt away, led off into the wilderness, abandoned utterly, with the sins of the people on his back, never to return to the camp. The Church has both of Israel's scapegoats on its hands: the sacrificial lamb without blemish and the one who bears our betrayal out of sight. For behind the hanging, twisting, early-bloating body of the dead Judas with its blackened face is the text, the galling text: "Then the disciples *all* forsook him and fled."

Jesus knows: Judas is standing in for somebody here. Do you remember it? Peter and all the others end up smelling like a rose—and so do we. We have our scapegoats too, for we cannot bear a redemption we do not deserve. This is why the *Crucible of Redemption* must open with the "Company of Betrayers." This is also why confession is such a difficult task for us. Is there any other kind of redemption than an undeserved redemption? This is the company of betrayed betrayers out of which he will build his kingdom and his Church. And who is our Judas now? Who and what do we use to qualify ourselves as God's deserving people? In contrast to whom are we clean, white and a dollar a yard? Who is this that hangs in our view; whose presence is used to make our betrayal look good? The same dread reality keeps demanding new Judases—*we just never could stand to be guilty.*

In a contemporary play the leading lady plans to

sacrifice herself by donating her only kidney to save
her son's life, because she can't bear to have the
shame of the child's parentage revealed. An old doctor says to her, "You would destroy your own life and
deprive your husband and son of your presence all
to save your foolish pride." And it is so. We just
can't stand being guilty. We never could. We never
could believe he really accepts us, guilt and all, as
we are. We all have to bring a little plea. We have
to have our Judas. We never could really believe the
words, "Yea, though thou art in thy blood yet have
I loved thee with an everlasting love." It never got
through. Consequently, we can hardly confess ourselves. And we can rarely accept ourselves. We keep
trying to create images that divert and justify. We
keep forgetting that the Church of God created
Judas' character to bear its sins away.

The Church of our fathers has continued to help
make new Judases to bear our sins away: the Jews
in Spain, in England, in modern Germany and Po-
land—throughout the extra long years of this "terrible twentieth century"—and it gets no better. Indeed,
it was no different with our grandfathers. Who taught
field hands they had no time to wash and didn't need
to marry to have children? Who taught field hands
that sanitation wasn't a problem in the fields? Who
taught field hands that fatback and weevilly flour

and dandelion greens were good enough, better than garden vegetables? And what state had on its books less than seventy-five years ago a law that says there is no crime against the person of a Negro that is a crime? Who created hate, and who now uses his created image of the Negro to damn him to hell further still? What Church of God is saying: *"These are our people; these are of us"*? We shaped them economically, geographically, spiritually, and physically. This is our Judas.

Or again, in a lesser but even more general way: on my kitchen wall there hangs a griznoid motto (griznoid is a local high school word that means anything terrible you want it to mean). It says:

> Dear Children, *father is always right:*
> stupid, uninformed, feeble-minded perhaps,
> but *always right!*

Now, what is it I ask you, what is it about us fathers that makes us unable to bear our own guilt so that we impose our godhood on our children to such an extent that they can never stand to be guilty either? We are this people. We just can't stand guilt. City councils can't stand it; mayors deny it; presidents denounce, to keep it from settling on them. The Ku Klux Klan accuses to stop accusations; churches blame sociology; nations blame neighbors—why must

we all always be like driven snow, white like angels?
What is this terrible urge we have for guiltlessness?
We are guilty here. Is not this the ground upon
which all redemption begins? Redemption is for us
guilty. It's a false craving that has to put our guilt
out of sight.

Let us begin this Holy Week by being able at least
to admit today that *the company of the glad is also
the company of the guilty.* And who, pray, needs
redemption more in our time than we who have
worshiped so many gods that are damned and so many
idols that are hollow? Let us begin with a prayer for
the grace to be glad that we too are among the
company of the guilty for whom Christ died.

The
Unavoidable
Cup

*"O my Father, if it be possible, let
this cup pass from me."*

As we walked along home from service she said,
"What have you done to Judas here?" The implica-
tions were many. She said, "Did you not make him a
dark Christ figure essential to our oneness?" Or,
"Must the Church always carry two scapegoats? Must
we really be grateful to Judas, too?" A dozen hearers
thanked me for cleaning up Judas—though that was
not my intention! And one startled me, utterly, by
saying at the door, "I knew a man named Judas."
(I had said only one kind of animal is ever named
Judas.) She said, "I knew a man named Judas"—

and I braced. Then she added, "He was a train robber"—and I relaxed.

Have I done a dangerous thing to Judas and to us? Indeed so. But we do not create a Judas cult. Judas is no dark Christ. Judas is not necessary to our atonement. Judas, rather, is the typification of our need and guilt—not its justification. Judas is never Saint Judas. If he were, this would sanctify every dark magic, every deep sorcery, every witchcraft, every bloody Mass that has ever appeared in religion's name. Judas is no Saint Judas. Judas is victim; Judas is sufferer; he is not wayfarer, viator, victor. Judas is there but Judas is not a pilgrim. Judas goes nowhere. He is a roadside execution and represents no victory. Judas is tragedy. Judas is *metamelomai,* remorse, but he is not *metanoia,* repentance. If Judas had turned, what a reconciling! But no scapegoat turns. He loses his character as scapegoat if he turns. Scapegoat is not scapegoat if he comes back to camp. He did not turn and we must let him go. Out of the week he is gone now, and the light will shift to the sacrificial lamb. We do not forget Judas; he is just not onstage anymore. For the light turns now to the altar and the sacrificial lamb, and stops. There isn't any redemption in a Judas death, only sorrow and darkness. He, Judas, was victim, just as any other is victim, but he was not viator. He had no way through. He was not wayfarer, though his cup seemed as unavoidable as ours.

So we had two lambs: at the altar and in the wilderness. And one is gone and the light now swings to the altar lamb, and stays there.

Lamb at the altar; lamb in the wilderness. How long they had acted these things out with lambs. These searing, visual images of redemption; these bloody, stumbling bearers of a hope of atonement with their little throats cut; these longing, reaching quests for oneness; this millennium-old craving to be right; Israel's eagerness to be rid of guilt; this wholesale flight from Sartre's "flies rolling down our throats in clusters," the flies of guilt that are everywhere. With ideas so powerful and universal; with symbols so moving and searing; with poetry like this Jewish symbolism, this drama with dumb symbols that could only bleat their responses; with this thousand-year-old Passover slaying for guilt's sake (Josephus counted over 248,000 lambs slaughtered in the Passover feasts in Jerusalem in the year 70) ; with these bleeding lambs—it was impossible but that sooner or later the place of the lamb would be acted out. For a little lamb would not do as a symbol forever.

Our great symbols are nearly always *acted out*. Our great ideas sooner or later are *person*ified. Abra-

ham Lincoln was offered the way of race extermination for Negroes in 1863—this would solve the con-
traband problem that Grant and others were facing
—but he turned away from the notion of mass extermination in a shuddering horror. Less than eighty
years later there came a man mad enough to act out
the symbolic idea of race extermination. The modern
so-called sex revolution is a wholesale acting out of
symbols of a dark and secret craving for freedom
and license. Anglo-Saxon pride is a tribal provin-
cialism—a very small tribe in a very small province
by the way—but now being acted out as a white
nationalism. The thirst for power and mobility now
symbolized with 300 horsepower machines is acted
out in the pitiless highway slaughter of thousands.
These great powers are nearly always acted out on
stage somewhere. A lamb would not do forever.
Sputnik's dog or the monkey put in Ranger I were
not enough to inhabit space—a *man* had to go in
orbit sooner or later. And so it was. A lamb couldn't
do forever. History being history, and symbols being
symbols, someone must go on the altar wherever our
symbols are taken seriously.

Human sacrifice is ultimately an unavoidable idea
in sacrificial faith systems. From Mexico to Asia
Minor the ceremonies that began with the crushing
of wheat in the mystery religions wound up sooner

or later in the crushing of life. What terrible power ordains this I do not know. I simply do not know. But all of a sudden in dark Gethsemane a chalice, a bedewed, dripping chalice shines like a jewel, filled with a dark and bitter brew, and the lamb shrinks back:

"Father, if it be possible, let this cup pass."

And in Matthew, stone silence. No ministering angel. No disciples hovering over. No voice from the blue to comfort. Matthew has it right according to my experience. When you cry sharpest, the answer is what Ignatius called it, *sige*—utter, stark silence. "Father, if it be possible . . . ." Silence.

Again the cry to avoid, "If this cannot pass unless I drink it . . . ." But what made him think it would pass if he did drink it? "If this cannot pass except I drink it . . . ." What made him think it would pass if he did drink it—it would choke him. Judas drank his cup and nothing passed—it was a dead end. What is this incredible notion that a cup like this will pass if you drink it?

And you—with your unavoidable cup that has loss in it or grief in it or death in it, and guilt in it and need in it and despair in it—what makes you think such a cup will pass if you drink it? Victim or viator? All of us are—victim. Some of us are both victim and wayfarer. Only for those who are both victim and wayfarer, passing through, will it pass. But you see, I don't know how old you have to be to know this—I have met people who know it and are very young. The difference is not in the cup that is there; the difference is not in the draught that is in the cup; the difference is not in the brew; the difference is not in whether you sip it or quaff if off. Some I have watched drink death like a toast to life, and I've never accustomed myself to seeing men drink death like a toast. Some drink death like a terrible emetic that disgorges as it goes down. But the difference? *The difference is in the drinker, not the drink.* All our unavoidable cups are fatal brews.

These drinkers of unavoidable cups, these who pass the cup. . . . The ability to pass the cup is in the drinker not the drink—he is viator and victim. Christ turns dark to light and night to day, but he cannot pass this cup by avoiding it. He-you, viator-wayfarer, can pass this cup only by quaffing it.

And you—which are you? Victim who stops here or wayfarer who goes through? We are both, I hope. But we do not yet know, do we? We are amateurs here.

I heard a man describe a terrible seventeen-hour vigil in which he watched over his own stricken corpse alone but was not afraid, was grateful not to be afraid, and was not really alone. He willed his suffering into life. The difference is in the drinker, and we all have our cup. Suddenly it gleams there in your Gethsemane, and you can't take your eyes off it. You shrink back—but you take and drink all of it, for the only way to pass it is to drink it. And life beyond becomes something in your hands too.

You will notice this week that Christ never turned back again. There is nothing else from which he shrinks. He is viator. He is headed through this. And this is why the light stays on him.

Which Man —
This Cross?

*"Which of the two will ye that I
release?" They said, "Barabbas."*

If salvation could ever be in a cross alone, there have
been enough crosses to save the world a million times
over. There were crosses cheek by jowl a single day
in a Roman arena. So thick the crosses were that
their arms had to be staggered; they overlapped.
There were crosses for miles on a Roman road when
an army revolted. And there are other kinds of
crosses: for many years the highest per capita death
rate for heart attacks was recorded for Negro mothers
who largely bore the burden of the family's anxiety.
Many an Irish or Indian mother has suffered enough
for a crucifixion. Many a smothered child in a nice

29

house, many a frustrated father, knows about crucifixion. If salvation were in a cross alone, there have
been enough crosses to have saved the world a million
times over.

But salvation cannot come from crosses only. Salvation can come only from a cross whose incumbent
hanging there has some future. Salvation has to come
from someone a cross cannot hold. Salvation has to
come from someone of whom a cross cannot dispose.
Salvation has to come from a cross we cannot forget,
a cross from which we cannot walk away. Salvation
cannot come from crosses that end something. Salvation has to come from that rare cross that is the
beginning of something.

So, really, between Jesus and Barabbas there was
no choice. The choice between Barabbas and Jesus
is empty and nigh meaningless. It's only there at all
because the Church, between A.D. 70 and 80, smart-
ing over the accusation of cowardice made by the
Jews, fled in mass from Jerusalem's fall. That gave
the early Church more reason to blame the Jews.
They remembered it into the book. They remembered all they had to make the Jews look guiltier.
But there really was no choice between Barabbas
and Jesus. Who could really have chosen Barabbas
against the teacher?

I think it was the awful silence of Jesus that did it. It just tore things up at that hearing. Nothing can provoke a judge like a prisoner who simply will not say anything. Not anything. The Revised Standard Version gives it: "The governor wondered greatly." I wonder if it doesn't better read, "The governor blew his stack!" A prisoner standing there with all these charges who says nothing! The charges pile up. He scorns reply. The accusations mount against him, and he inspects his fingernails. How provoking—an accused one who cannot even hear the accusations. So Pilate, provoked, offers a choice, a phony choice, an empty choice, a pointless choice. For one of these has no eligibility for a death that helps anybody. He's eligible for death—who isn't? But he has no eligibility for a death that helps. He simply is no candidate. He has no prospect to offer. For there is no salvation in any crucified one unless he has a future, and Barabbas, living or dying, had no future. Whether he lived or died, he had no future. And Pilate flings out this empty choice.

Suppose they had said, "Give us Jesus." Suppose they had said, "Crucify Barabbas!"—it would have made no difference. We Jews, we Romans, we Britons, we Americans—we would have corrected our choice later. It would have made no difference. Some of us, history being what it is, would have got to him.

Barabbas is not eligible. For the story's sake Barabbas is a prop. He cannot offer us anything that matters. So they said, "Give us Barabbas. . . . Crucify Jesus!" and Pilate washed his hands.

Let him wash. It makes no difference whether he washes or doesn't wash. Let him wash. How could Pilate have known that the crucified one had a future? No one else he had ever crucified had a future. And Pilate was plagued to death with the bloody Jews and their crazy nationalism. Mighty Rome had never been so patient; in four hundred years Rome had never been so patient as she had been with these bloody, stubborn Jews. Let Pilate go. He has served his turn.

Turn your glance instead to the chosen. Do you think it would have mattered that they chose Jesus? They couldn't have elected Jesus for this if God had not already chosen him, to back him. But this is the silence in Gethsemane. No hovering angel. No softening word. No private bootlegged surety. This is the meaning of the silence in Gethsemane. He has to die cold, just as you do, with no guaranteed future. There is no sub-rosa agreement in advance. "Father, if it be possible, let it pass . . ."—utter silence. So Israel chose whom God had chosen, or we would still have no crucifixion with a future.

Here at last, in Jesus the Christ, we have a proper

candidate. And what was new here, what was new about him? Let that grand liberal of fifty years ago, whom the great modern theologian, Karl Barth, rose up to challenge, let Harnack answer. *"Purity was new."* It was new then; it is new now. "Now the spring burst forth afresh, and broke a new way for itself through the rubbish." A pure man is new. And *personhood* was new. Did you ever in all your life come across any man who better knew his name? Have you ever seen anyone in all your life so sublimely sure he had a father? And that he knew his father's name? Personhood was new. "How utterly impossible," Ernst Troeltsch would say, "for it to have been that the community could have forgotten him. How utterly impossible it would have been for them *not* to experience a continuation with him." Indeed, Troeltsch's notion that the Holy Spirit himself is none other than the *Pneuma-Christ*—the spirit Christ—has never had a decent treatment in theology these thirty years. The *Pneuma-Christ*, the spirit Christ, is literally the Holy Spirit who could have taken no other form of manifestation to people than the way they had seen him. So they made a proper choice for crucifixion—as if they had anything to do with it that mattered. They elected him, as if it made any difference.

Oh, we would have got him cruxed someway. He

was a proper candidate: young, fair, clean, with eyes on a distant horizon. So fair was he that wherever we shall go among the planets of space, if men are found there, we shall be looking for one to match him above all men we have known. There is no other body we would be willing to compare men with, if we should meet them.

What kind of people are we men who always pick that kind to crucify? What kind of people are we, we men who crucify that kind? The innocent kind. The child kind. But listen to him say, "Weep not for me. Weep for yourselves." I was less than twenty when I began to live a life that has been an almost constant grief reaction; it is a cosmic grief; it is the existential sadness, that we should be everywhere men who crucify that kind. "Weep for yourselves."

Weep
Not
for Me

And there followed him a great company of the people and of women.

There always had been the women: at the wedding in Cana, in the Nazareth beginning, that night at Simon's house, both times at the house of Lazarus and at Lazarus' grave, at the Cross, at the tomb, on the Street of Sorrows—there always were the women. I will not go into this opening, why they are there. They are always there; faithfully there, helpfully there, frustratingly there, sorrowfully there, aesthetically there, needfully, redemptively, courageously —they are always there. They were hungrily there from the very first, when some overwrought freed-

woman cried out the first note of Mary worship:
"Blessed be the womb that bore thee; and the paps
that gave thee suck."

Who wouldn't wish to be his mother! They all
wanted him for a son. They all wanted him for a
son or a lover or a dream of both. There is always
a native homosexual beckoning in truly religious
figures: the feminine nature of the male in religion
and the masculine nature of the female leader—these
are always present, the feminine in rare proportions.
There was the grace, the acceptance, the receptivity,
the gentleness, the winsome remnant of the little
boy they would have cradled. There is a kind of
pious lesbian urge in religious fidelity that stands
around waiting, adoring, uniting with the feminine
in the masculine. But there was always more. For
always there were men standing by, too.

The women are there that day on the Via Dolorosa,
and seeing him so cross-bound their hearts break,
and he says, "Daughters of Jerusalem, weep not for
me." But we do. We must. We must weep at anything passing by so fair and so unfair. So high and
so lowly. Any contradiction like this tears us. This is
why only the rarest of our artists can show his beauty
without its spilling over into a kind of Anglo-Saxon
femininity. This is why that agony can hardly be
shown without slipping into maudlinity. This is why

the ugliness can scarcely be seen without distortion. Who can fail to weep at the contradiction? But there is a proper weeping even here.

How difficult it is to keep Easter without slushy sentiment. Better to let it go, some say, than to spill over it with slush—or is it? A friend said that if it were not for the Junior Chamber of Commerce fighting over who would sponsor the sunrise service, it wouldn't be Easter in Jackson this year. But we keep it here. We spend an eight-day week at it here. We put over a thousand man hours into it here. We print books and worship programs about it. We quit work and assemble. We bring gladly the singers and the preparation and the lilies and the symbols. We sit intently. We listen. We visit our neighbor and sister churches and we worship. We cluster around the grave and cross a week—we mean business here with our weeping—but starkly, too, we hear him say, "Weep not for me."

No annual weeping in some sanctuary does any good. No clustering up in little bands of women or men, no lingering in the pews to cry, no loitering over a prayer-band diversion. "Weep not for me"— don't hand him this seasonal splurge of tears and lament, this fever of reading devotional treatises. No memorial floral piece dropped tearfully on a mound of sorrows annually is either expiation for, or commitment to, anything that matters. No sermon tasting. No daily pilgrimage will do it. No Lenten diet. No theological binge. No embalming sentiment. No assembly of women at the well or women at a wedding or women at Lazarus' grave or at Christ's grave can make any difference to him or to us. For he, on his way through, for us and for our salvation says, "Weep not for me." But there is a proper weeping.

"Weep for yourselves and for your children." And what could that mean except this: if you are going to cry, cry about the same things he cried about. Turn your eyes upon the object of his weeping. Identify with the reason he was sacrificed. If you weep, weep for that which makes God weep. Join that lonely cry in Samuel Miller's libretto for the oratorio *What Is Man?* Here the great God Almighty sees his creature turning away from him, and God sends up and out that heartbroken cry, *"Adam!"*

Weep that we always did reverse things. We always did foul the cup; profane the holy. Weep even for the animals, says Father Zossima in *The Brothers Karamazov,* "who do not soil the earth as we men do."

So, we weep for lost dimensions, over swamps we and our fathers and grandfathers created; we weep for a culture we dare not abandon because we know nothing created by us would replace it. Weep, if you wish, that you cannot redeem yourself. Weep that we wear his name and not his power. Weep for politicians. Weep for white racists. Weep for Negro hate and neighborhood scandal and crime and ignorance. Weep for slavery magnified with gadgets. And weep for Mount Zion, shrouded there in the mist, but always in our reach. Weep for Viet Nam and South Mississippi and Washington Heights in Charlotte. Weep for Watts, Detroit, Newark, and old Brooklyn. Weep for our history and our future. And more —weep for the children. For always in the Scriptures, since Jeremiah at least, the children of the desolate, the abandoned wife's children, have been more numerous than the children of the marriage. There is a proper weeping. He turns us toward it.

This is the ecumenical sorrow that Angus Dun used to remind us of at the World Council. One weeps for that which made it worth it for him to die. You weep for his weeping. If you do not, you haven't joined. If you do not, you are not connected. One of our great crimes is that we have been diverted from our crosses by his cross, and there is no salvation in that. When he says, "Save your weeping for yourselves," it means: join him in his agonizing concerns. It means: you, too, must weep over a village you cannot take.

"O Jerusalem, Jerusalem, how oft would I have

gathered thee"—this is the gospel of redemption. If his weeping becomes your weeping, then his cup becomes a common chalice with your cup. We are to drink it together and weep for the same things. But beneath it he will let us, I think, keep a tear. He will let us weep that he could save others but not himself. He couldn't, and be the saver. I think we can still weep for that.

The Impossible Salvation

"He saved others; let him save himself if he is the Christ of God, the Chosen One."

And he could not. We still must weep, I think, for that. For what? That the chosen ones of God always seem to have such a hard time of it. Isn't this the Holy Scripture's only problem? Isn't this the Holy Scripture's real purpose—theodicy? Isn't the unfinished task of the Holy Scripture to make our God look good, to justify the so-called ways of God to those who can't stand the way he does? ✓

In all our experience with the Judeo-Christian faith, the ones we keep remembering, the chosen ones, the favored ones, the endued and endowed

41

ones, the anointed ones, always, uniformly, always
have such a hard time of it. According to the record,
according to our memories as a community, *the
chosen one nearly always gets it.* Old-time infantry
men who survived lived this out, and they had a
rule: *only a fool volunteers.* "Volunteers always get
plastered," they say—therefore never volunteer. Volunteers get mentioned in dispatches but their medals
are always awarded posthumously. It is so with God's
volunteers too. His chosen nearly always get it.

This says something about God, doesn't it? It says
that God is a very poor picker. Or, it says that God is
a pretty sorry backer. It says that God does not care
for justice much, that God's chosen ones always get
it. It seems to say either that God is stupid or that
God is weak or that God is blind. In any case, it has
seemed pretty dangerous to get "chosen." And who
can justify the ways of God to man? Who can justify
the way God operates with Job? Who can justify the
way God operates with Hosea? Who can make what
happened to King David's children look good? Who
can clean up Isaiah's "Suffering Servant"? Who can
save Zerubbabel? Who can help Jonah? Or Moses? Or
Israel? Why must God's chosen always get blasted?
This problem gnawed at Israel's vitals all her history.
Why does God's picked one always get it?

There was perfectly moral ground for this question

to be raised at crucifixion. It takes this form: if you can save, save; save yourself. If you would save yourself you might even save God. For if you come down from *that* cross, we will put God back where he belongs again. We will believe again. You could save God if you would save yourself. For God is in trouble everywhere. He's in trouble for what always happens to his chosen one.

Everybody there saw it. Everybody there remembered it. It is the old curse against God: *the cry for God to look good just once.* It is the cry for God to win one—instead of losing them all. It is the cry for God to make sense. It is the cry for the Divine to come out in the open where we can see him. It is the cry for him to show his right arm and say what he's up to instead of leaving us to flounder so. It is the cry for God to be brave, for God to be just according to our notion of justice. *It is the cry for God to get on the side of his own people and not be so damned impartial!* It is the cry for God to be good to us. It's the demand that if God is chooser, defender, blesser, preserver, and saver—then let him defend, bless, preserve, and save the ones he has chosen.

It has hardly been a week since you thought it. When you turned that terrible corner and the cup was there before you, you thought, why me? What have I done to deserve this? Why does God do this way? He knows I believe anyhow. Or you thought, all I have ever said to fellow sufferers in this situation is now a silly platitude that doesn't apply to me at all. Or you thought, there is no word in faith that can comfort me. And I, myself, turn to Ecclesiastes. There is nothing else to read. A wire from my friend Bobby Bell to one dear says: "God must know what he's doing—we surely don't."

It's an old one, sure enough, the perfectly proper wish that God would make sense once. And the refusal to answer on God's part has made many a decent agnostic like myself become an indecent agnostic like myself. What concessions I have to make to believe! What concessions of self and values a man must give to believe in God at all—because it goes too hard with God's volunteers. "Come down," they say. "Come down from the cross and we will believe."

Will we now? If he comes down, will we? Will we believe if our God accepts our definition of good? Will we believe just because he is good to us? Is God's goodness really dependent upon his picking me out? We are all liars, the Book says. The Book says we wouldn't believe if one came home from the dead— and so he doesn't bother with our petty objections. He came not down. He couldn't. For there is a heavy reality here to be borne by us all. The decision not to come down had focused long before. It happened at the temptations. In that confrontation with Satan, the adversary, he had spurned that "Cast thyself down from the temple, his angels will bear thee up. Come down and we will believe." Here it is really acted out from the cross, and he will not abandon the vehicle. He will ride it through or perish forever. And so it was.

Is there a deeper explanation? I certainly think so. And I'm sure it includes his chosen ones as well, all of them. It was acted out previously, months before, when Christ's own nearest and dearest sent an agitated message. John the Baptizer, in dungeon, his head forfeit, sends to say, "Are you really he, or must we look for some other? Any other! Do your job, Messiah! Throw off your disguise!" And Jesus sent a message, "Tell John, happy is that fellow who does not stumble all over me." "John, dear John," the heart message said, "you wonder at my method, why I leave you there"—and the heart talk rises clear and sharp—"John, listen to me; I can no more come to you than I can come down from my own cross. In the wilderness I could not turn stones to bread. In your death I cannot save you. In my death I cannot save me—not and be true to the mission."

Do you now see who is pushing Jesus through Gethsemane? John the Baptizer is behind him and it's a scandal. God's scandal; that the saver has to be so needy of saving himself. That the crucified must really be the victim of an impossible salvation. That God has to get in on it too. And stumble as we will, we cannot pass this unless it is really true.

Everything that lives, lives only by running the risks of living. Everyone who gives birth, every mother, runs the gauntlet. Every teacher who is a teacher, teaches himself away. Every doctor who is a curer, rather than a mere healer, gives himself in driblets. Every brother loses himself in a brother. And unless God is a God who will die to save us, we cannot be saved. And I cannot answer this yet. Perhaps this is how it can be "the blood shed for many."

A little boy who cannot answer his own crucifixion of two weeks ago told his mother night before last, "Marney can't satisfy my questions, but they are quieter now, for I notice he keeps dropping by to see if I am still all right." Maybe so. Maybe we have to keep dropping by Golgotha to see if God is still there, so that our crucifixion is all right.

The Blood
Shed
for Many

Maundy Thursday

Following our discovery that the saver can never be saved, that God has joined him in his dying, following this, have you just dropped by Church to see if God is still all right? To see if the Crucified One has come down? To see if he has come down from the cross so that we can believe?

Well, he is not there on the cross, but he did not come down. He never came down. He was *taken* down. He was *received* down, in a blessed *pieta*. Left to him, he would still be there. Life just ran out on him. And what good is a corpse on a cross? He was taken down, but he never came down—and the cross is empty.

A friend of mine tells me that the archaeologist Romanoff uncovered what, to him, was indisputable evidence that behind the rubbish of the third wall the Lord's own grave had been found, but he had been persuaded not to publish for the sake of the people it would harm! I said, "Rubbish! Let him publish! Let him publish all he knows! It couldn't hurt. For this is not where he said he would meet us. Not under any wall. Find the old wood of the cross; find all kinds of graves—this is not where he would meet us. He said he would meet us at neither cross nor grave; he said he would meet us at his table."

Broken body, shed blood, done for all and for all times, and he meets us here. Don't you think he comes thirsty to the table? Eager to the table? Eager for the new wine he said he would drink with us, too, in his Father's kingdom. Welcome then, all you who have come to see if he is here. For two thousand years he has been coming, and we have been coming —we of the Church—to see if he is here. Come then—all you who do intend to live in charity and concord with your neighbor and are willing to repent

yourself and forsake your sins and turn to the for-
giving fellowship of Christ as you meet it in your
brethren. And let us take counsel. And let us remember. And let us expect. And let us meet him
in the Supper.

Beginning of maundy Thursday!

The
Bottom of
the Cup

"It is finished."

Most times the Church has distorted its great memories and experiences in the very act of remembering them. In our remembering we keep mixing up the time and the place sequence. We keep introjecting what we learned later into earlier events to keep the earlier event from hurting so. We keep expecting ideas the Church had no notion about, ideas that came as total surprise, to meliorate, or soften, the hard realities of the earlier experience that came before the ideas were really present. Or to put it more plainly—we keep forcing the Church

50

to use the New Testament before it was written. We keep expecting the Church to have at its disposal what it couldn't have caught yet.

For example, in the conversations following each of these sermons I've kept hearing a keen disappointment. It is as if you felt bereft of something. But that's the way we ought to be. There is no relief for Calvary's death before Easter. Any ray of hope in the New Testament account was hindsight. He came into it cold.

I hear you; you keep wanting to deny his manhood. I hear you wanting him to shift gears and be different. I hear you wanting him to have his cake and eat it. It is a way you have of saying it wasn't really death—he knew beforehand. I hear you saying he really didn't die. He had advance information. He knew about. . . . I hear you expecting me to do this too: to bootleg resurrection before Calvary, to let him pull his rank on us and not die as we die, limited by our resources.

Now you may do this if you insist—the Church has committed this crime a long time. You may do this if you insist. You may put resurrection right in the middle of the Last Supper, but it's a distortion. You may put it in the triumphal entry; you may put your resurrection in the cleansing of the temple; you may use it on the Street of Sorrows, and you may insert it between all but one of the last words. You may put it in the Tower of Babel if you need it there. You may put it into the Garden of Eden —and some have. But I think we are old enough now to face the cost if we do. *If you put resurrection into Holy Week you empty atonement because you destroy incarnation.* You make his death a death done for himself and for God but not for me, or the many. You make his death a play performed with nothing at stake because it is done so unlike the death of the many. You make it a death by itself, in a class to itself, and it does not participate in our death if you give him advance information. You empty his death of its redemptiveness if you do this. If he does not come into it cold too, you make his death a farce because he did not really die. It's a docetic disgrace if you do this.

But, you say, the New Testament accounts show that he was preparing them for his death with foregleams of resurrection. And you are right. There are foregleams all over the place! But they could not really hear them then. They never heard them until after the Easter event. They could not receive his resurrection because they did not yet believe in his death! And this is where we are. You have to believe in the death first. And no legitimate, charismatic utterance can relieve you of this.

Real, unrelieved, this it was—Black Friday. And the fact of unrelieved death overbore anything they remembered of resurrection. It always does when you first believe in death. The despair belongs here. It is just like this with your deaths. I know it is just like this with your deaths. If a pious neighbor comes in within the hour, or if your pastor comes, or if the Church's liturgy and teaching are brought in, or some old family connection comes rushing in with old odd pieces torn out of Holy Writ and begins to say to you, "God must have loved him so much he took him," you say, "What kind of God is that!" If they say, "In his resurrection body he is so much better off," you say, "How could he be better off than with me?" If they say, "He is happy now," you say, "It's an adultery for him to be happy anywhere else except with me." Or if they say, "You will meet again," you say, "I don't think so." You can't hear this word. You will not have the word of resurrection yet. You curl your lip inside at this pious fraud. You turn away. You hear it as a pious imposition. You will not have it! Why? Because you can't even see his death yet, much less the beyond death. You cannot stand the thought of death yet. So it's much better when your pastor comes, for him to have nothing to say. It's much better to bring a dish of something, much better. Just bring a dish and sit. Do that. There is no faith in resurrection possible before you have accepted death.

This is why these messages have been so bleak. It is three days later at your house before the worship service can begin—"I am the resurrection and the life, he that believeth in me though he were dead. . . ." There, sometimes, three days later, you can begin to hear—if you are not so tranquilized with chemicals you neither feel nor know.

Indeed, he had told them this beforehand, but they couldn't hear it. They did not yet believe in his death. And it was only in the blessed afterward that they could recall and put the foregleams in the record. So on Good Friday no resurrection word is to be said. For here we have come to believe in the death for the many.

And here we learn again that, with all its mysteries, the Church cannot say both its great wonders in the same breath. It has been twenty years since one could preach divinity and humanity in the same sermon. One can hardly say miraculous birth and real humanity in the same sermon. One can hardly say Son of God, Son of man, in the same moment. I can't say life except as I have experienced death. And I cannot say resurrection and cross together until I have said them *one at a time as things happen*. And this is why the most important printer's symbol in

the whole alphabet of printer's symbols becomes the
hyphen. We keep having to use it to tie our irrecon-
cilables together: I-thou, life-death, light-dark.

This is the threat—that these great opposites may
cancel each other out. Cross-resurrection may cancel
each other out, you say, and we shall be left with
the threat and the burden of meaninglessness. Indeed
we shall! You are too adult to avoid it any longer.
For here only, where we are driven to our knees, do
we "meet the God who appears when God has dis-
appeared in the anxiety of our doubts." Matthew
puts it: "He gave up the ghost." Mark puts it: "He
gave a cry and died." Luke puts it: "Father, into thy
hands." And John says: "It is finished."

It has to be really finished, it has to be *really*
finished, before God who is God can appear. And
from here, on Black Friday, we can only wait. For
this is where he was driven in that final word in
Luke: "Father, into thy hands." If there is any more
it is God's. And that is why, if you ask, all the claims
the Church can make are still by hindsight. Some
things we learn from looking back over our shoulder.
This is the bottom of the cup of redemption.

Once at All Saints Church, at the ordination of
an old friend, I knelt to receive communion. Dying
on his feet with Hodgkin's disease, with a new Ph.D.
from Chicago hanging around his neck, being or-

dained into a "foreign" priesthood, he gave us wine; and when he came to me, the cup was almost empty. Over my shoulder, as we went away from the altar, I saw him, dead these seven years now, I saw him turn the chalice up to get the last ruby drop himself. But he drank it really long before, as did our Lord, from the bottom of his cup.

The Lord
Hath Reigned
from
the Tree

We are, I am sure, all of us here out of some great wish to believe. Perhaps there is more expectancy of resurrection *here* than there was *there*. For when resurrection burst into the midst of the disciples, it found them headed out on different journeys, and it was as if they had been caught from the rear by some unspeakably good news. For the uniform note of reaction to resurrection on the part of his associates was total surprise. So far as I can tell, none of his disciples expected it.

Of course the Scripture says he had told them

earlier; they had some foregleams which, if he really said them, they were remembering and inserting much later; but whatever he may or may not have said about resurrection, or whatever he knew to say, *they had not heard it.* They did not even then believe in his death, much less his resurrection. And now his death was a brutal fact. It stunned like a blow. It was all they could stand. The wrenching and unrelieved agony of his going so suddenly from them dominated everything. Except for Peter himself, who had a terrible extra burden, for he was horribly, personally, agonizingly shamed—like a beaten dog of some kind he hid under a porch floor unrelievedly ashamed and bereft. And besides, undoubtedly by now someone had come across the body of Judas, so all they could feel was the collapse of everything.

It had gone so swiftly from the supper: arrest, trial, crucifixion, dead before dark—they couldn't take it in. Arrest, trial, crucifixion, in the grave before dark. They were utterly bereft. So far as I know, none of them looked for resurrection. What words he had said were not even remembered or were not meant to be believed. Any warning of resurrection they had, had gone glimmering off into the unconscious like play darts made out of paper, thrown by little boys over some high bluff into the dark. This is always our situation when resurrection comes. All of our great redemptions have always come up on us from the rear.

But not a one expected it, so far as we know. Not a single disciple lay there in the shrubbery alongside the grave waiting, waiting, waiting, to see. Not a single one. If this were not so, if it were not so that nobody expected it, Mary would have gone for a different purpose than to bring some embalming fluid. Peter and John would not have been where they would have to run to get to the tomb. The two would not have been going to Emmaus at all, and the story of the women would not have seemed an idle tale to the disciples. There would have been no going back to fishing for a living nor any distant gathering of disciples in an upper room. If they had expected resurrection, they would have been, as we would have been, at the tomb's lip waiting for the first stirrings of that bound body, and they would have had Lazarus on their arm. I don't know whatever happened to Lazarus—but they neither believed nor remembered nor expected, no more than you do, really. They just grieved and went on to live their shattered remnants, and they had no right to do this. Had he not taught them for three years that faith is hope? But faith had died and so had hope, and resurrection had to come up on them from the rear. He had to come to them. He almost always does.

Have you heard that faith without works is dead? Faith without hope is not faith either. For dead faith, faith you once had, is not faith. And the disciples were not sustained by any bogus notion, by any imitation idea of eternal life available to everybody and popular with us. They didn't have our Greek cemetery ideas, our Rest Lawns. These are biblical people. They are not Greek savants—they are peasants. They are not philosophers. And they had no notion of an eternity which belongs to the man, "an eternity which man essentially possesses in himself," as Emil Brunner puts it. They had no idea of an eternity which a man can recognize as his own true being. They had no real personal eternity yet. Just how the cool darkness of Sheol fit them, or how the flashing and quick destruction of Gehenna, the city dump, affected them, I do not know. But these are biblical people and they had no vague, general notion of immortality, really.

This is why they were eligible for resurrection. If they had had such a notion, the other resurrection couldn't have got to them. Those of you who already have some kind of vague eternity as a fact of human existence miss the point altogether, and are not eligible for the Christian resurrection. Resurrection comes to you only when you have no substitute.

You've never heard a more biblical notion than this. For the Bible does not speak of an eternity which man essentially possesses in himself and which he can recognize as his own true *ontos,* or being. It speaks rather of the eternity that comes to man, eternal life which lays hold of him, which is bestowed upon him.

Now what kind of man does it take to withstand being flayed alive? What kind of men does it require to be cruxed, drowned, pulled in four pieces by wild horses, crossed by the thousand? Do you think the kind we have watched skulking in the darkness of their utter defeat could do this? Yes. That's the only kind he had. They could do this, the same men, when resurrection, whatever it was, came to them. It is incredible how all the eight resurrection appearances act this out. Resurrection is not a given for everything that lives, only death is given. Resurrection comes to the receiver.

And so, through the seaside mist he comes to them. On the road to Emmaus he comes to them. And when they are gathered in the upper room or again on the day of Pentecost, he comes to them. Resurrection still does come if you receive it. The only eternal life Scripture knows anything about is eternal life which comes to you. And beginning here, where you are, if you receive it, changes everything. They found the quality of the eternal irrepressibly in their lives; it had to come to them.

Now, and in later years, as they answered and remembered and liturgicized their experiences, they never forgot the dreadful day before resurrection had come to them, that terrible cross day. And gradually in the light of their subsequent experiences with him, gradually in the light of the increasing number of their own crosses, they came to revalue the cross day and to say, "It was while he was on his tree, before the resurrection, that he was at his greatest." They began to say, "The cross day was the day of days." From the tree they saw the womb of their resurrection and began to say of Good Friday: *"This too is the day the Lord hath made;* this was the day containing all our days. It was from there, crucifixion, that the height was scaled and resurrection was contained. This is the highwater mark."

Earlier than I can find, in some ancient liturgy, earlier than the Saint James, or the Saint Mark, or the third-century Greek liturgies at least, the congregation began to give a response in words like this:

The Lord hath reigned from the tree.

They meant that highwater mark of his crucifixion to look toward, to leap forward, and contain within it, the promise of everything that would follow. It just may be that way with yours and mine. It is from the tree that he reigns.

But I did find something in the old Saint James Liturgy I did not know, or had forgotten: that in order to say this at their high Mass, instead of giving everyone a wafer and a sip, they dipped dry bread in the chalice with the wine and soaked it so that the participant took both at once, remembering that it was from the tree that life was given and the reign was begun.

The Lord hath reigned from the tree.